A New True Book

THE MENOMINEE

By Joan Kalbacken

CHILDRENS PRESS®

CHICAGO

Menominee artwork decorates
a viaduct in Neopit, Wisconsin.

Project Editor: Fran Dyra
Design: Margrit Fiddle

AP/Wide World Photos–37 (left)

The Bettmann Archive–23 (top), 27

© Reinhard Brucker–7; Wisconsin State
Museum, 8, 14, 17 (bottom left), 19 (inset),
21 (right), 33 (left); Milwaukee Public
Museum, 13, 16 (left), 23 (bottom), 24;
Field Museum, Chicago, 16 (right), 20,
22 (right)

Courtesy of Ada Deer–© David Loeb, 37
(right)

Tom Dunnington–map on page 7

© Joan Kalbacken–26

North Wind Picture Archives–9, 17 (right),
21 (left), 31, 32

Courtesy of the Oshkosh Public Museum,
Oshkosh, Wisconsin. All rights reserved.–
29 Neg #1836

Root Resources–© Jim Nachel, Cover, 2,
33 (right), 39 (left & top right), 40
(2 photos), 42, 43 (left), 45 (left); © Gail
Nachel, 39 (bottom right), 43 (right), 45
(right)

Tom Stack & Associates–© Tom Stack, 17
(top left)

The State Historical Society of Wisconsin–
5 Neg #18851, 15 Neg #24965, 19 Neg
#19690, 22 (left) Neg #32815, 34 Neg
#32808

Valan–© Phillip Norton, 18; © Michel
Bourque, 18 (inset)

COVER: Menominee Tribal Powwow
Grand Entrance

Library of Congress Cataloging-in-Publication Data

Kalbacken, Joan
   The Menominee / by Joan Kalbacken.
      p.   cm.–(A New true book)
   Includes index.
   ISBN 0-516-01054-9
   1. Menominee Indians–History–Juvenile literature.
2. Menominee Indians–Social life and customs–Juvenile
literature. [1. Menominee Indians. 2. Indians of
North America.] I. Title.
E99.M44K35   1994
973'.04973–dc20   93-36671
                                CIP
                                AC

TABLE OF CONTENTS

THE FIRST MENOMINEE

The Menominee believed in Māec-Awāetok, the Great Spirit and the Father of Fathers. Māec-Awāetok made the sun and the stars. He also made the earth and many spirit beings, giving them the form of animals. According to a Menominee legend, the Great Bear asked Māec-Awāetok to change him into a man. The Great Spirit granted his request.

The Menominee used this "Dream Dance Drum" in their ceremonies.

The man was alone, so
he asked a golden eagle
to come down and be his
brother. The two brothers
then asked a beaver to
join their family. She
became Beaver Woman.

5

Together they adopted a wolf, a crane, and a moose. All of them became human beings, and each adopted another member for the family. According to the legend, these were the first Menominee.

When Christopher Columbus came to the Americas in 1492, about 3,000 Menominee lived near the shores of Lake Michigan. The Menominee people were one of the

Map of the Menominee homeland   Lake Michigan at Cave Point, Wisconsin

Eastern Woodland tribes.
They lived near the mouth
of the Menominee River in
Wisconsin, among forests,
lakes, and streams. Today,
most Menominee still live
in the Midwest.

WILD RICE GATHERERS

The name *Menominee* comes from *Menominiwok,* an Indian word meaning "wild rice gatherers." Wild rice, a cereal grass, grows in the shallow lakes and streams around Lake

Cedar bark bags such as this one were used to store wild rice.

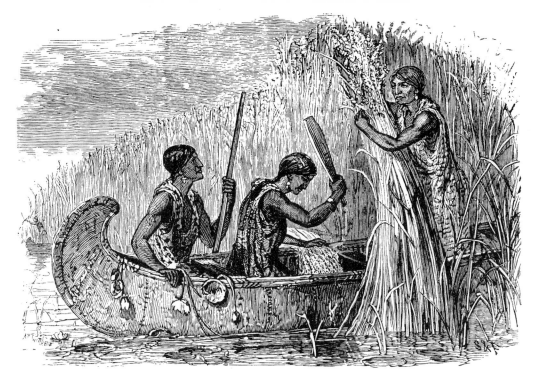

The Menominee pulled the wild rice stalks over the boat and knocked the grain into the canoe bottom.

Superior and Green Bay. Each fall, Menominee families gathered the wild rice in canoes. They boiled the grains and ate them with maple sugar. Some Menominee families still gather wild rice today.

GOVERNMENT

The Menominee nation is divided into two halves. One half is called Bear. The other is called Thunderer. Each half is made up of clans, or clusters of clans, who think of themselves as "Younger Brothers" to each other. These clan clusters are called "phratries." Membership in a clan is inherited through the father.

In the beginning, Thunderers were given fire and corn. The Bears were given wild rice. Each side must share its foods and gifts with the other.

Each phratry has a special knowledge or talent and a specific task. The Bear Phratry is made up of good speakers who are keepers of the Menominee laws. The Eagle Phratry works for freedom and justice.

Community life and safety are the work of the Moose Phratry. Artwork and building are the special skills of the Crane Phratry. And the Wolf Phratry has the best hunters and gatherers.

The tribal council chose the chief of the tribe from the Bear Phratry. The chief kept order, approved tribal decisions, and looked after the welfare of his people.

This museum scene shows a Menominee wigwam and birchbark canoe.

LIVING IN THE WOODLANDS

Menominee houses were used mainly for shelter, sleeping, and storing supplies. In good weather, cooking and eating were done outside.

Their winter homes were

This scene shows the inside of a wigwam.

wigwams built on a frame of wooden poles. First, the poles were placed in the ground in a circle. Then the tops of the poles were bent toward the center and tied with strips of soft bark. The wigwam was covered with cattail mats or birchbark.

Summer homes were built with poles placed in the shape of a triangle. These poles were not bent. They formed a high roof that helped keep the home cool. The families slept on the floor, on animal skins or grass mats.

Menominee children in front of their summer home

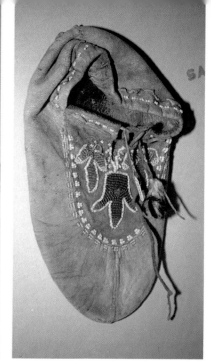

Traditional Menominee clothing, such as shirts (left) and moccasins, was made from animal skins. Often, it was decorated with colorful beads.

Hunting was important. The Menominee used the meat for food and the skins for clothing and mats. The hunters used smooth wooden bows rubbed with bear grease. Their pine or cedar arrows were decorated with hawk and eagle feathers.

16

The sturgeon (top left) was a favorite food fish. The Menominee used spears (bottom left) to hunt the fish from canoes (above).

The Menominee also caught fish from lakes, rivers, and streams. They fished with spears, hooks, and nets of bark. Their favorite fish was the sweet-tasting sturgeon.

17

Large maple trees grow in the Menominee woodlands. In spring, the Indians tap a hole in the trees. The sap drips into a pail hung beneath the

The sugar maple tree has very rich sap that can be boiled to make a sweet syrup or sugar. The sap is drained into pails hung on the trunk (inset).

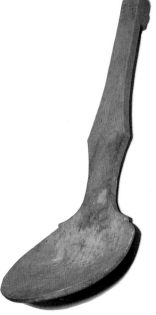

This painting (above) shows a camp of maple sugar makers.
The spoon (right) was used for scooping the sugar.

hole. The sap is boiled to
make a thick syrup. With
longer cooking, the syrup
turns into sugar. Today, the
Menominee sell maple
syrup and sugar.

CEREMONIES AND MEDICINE MEN

This bear claw bag was used in ceremonies honoring the bear spirit.

Bears are highly respected by the Menominee. In the early days, a special ceremony was held when a bear was killed. Friends were invited to a feast of bear meat. Invitations were carried by a messenger with a gift of tobacco. Native Americans believed that the spirits

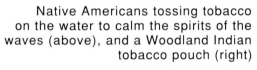
Native Americans tossing tobacco on the water to calm the spirits of the waves (above), and a Woodland Indian tobacco pouch (right)

liked tobacco and tobacco smoke. They threw tobacco on the water for the spirits before gathering wild rice.

The Menominee also respected Wabeno, the Morning Star Man. Wabeno

21

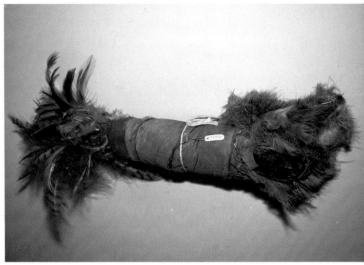

Louis Pigeon (left) was a Menominee medicine man. The Menominee charm (above) decorated with owl feathers was used by medicine men in healing ceremonies.

had the power to give health and long life, or sickness and death. They believed that a shaman, or medicine man, got his healing power from visions sent by the spirits.

In the game of lacrosse, each side was made up of many players. The teams used sticks to try to hit a ball into a goal. Below right: Lacrosse sticks and balls

GAMES AND FOLKTALES

Lacrosse was a favorite game. The Menominee used a ball made of deerskin and stuffed with hair. A racket was made from a three-foot sapling bent to form a cup. They played in honor of the Thunderbird.

Children rolled
birchbark hoops.
Girls played with
homemade dolls.
Boys had bows
and arrows.
During the long
winter months,
the families told
stories in
the wigwams.

Boy and girl dolls
made by the
Woodland Indians

SPIRIT ROCK

One legend tells about some Menominee warriors who asked the Great Spirit to grant their wishes. Most of the warriors asked for success in battle, in hunting, or in finding a wife. But one warrior asked for everlasting life. Such pride angered the Great Spirit. He granted the wish by changing the warrior into an everlasting stone–Spirit Rock.

Spirit Rock is a symbol for the Menominee people.

Spirit Rock is near Keshena Falls, Wisconsin. To this day, the Menominee believe that the rock is the tribe's symbol. If the rock ever crumbles away, there will no longer be a Menominee nation. Gifts of tobacco are still placed on top of the crumbling rock.

This painting shows Jean Nicolet arriving in Wisconsin.

EUROPEANS ARRIVE

In 1634, a French explorer named Jean Nicolet reported meeting Menominee people on the shores of Lake Michigan. The Native Americans and the French became good friends. The French traded clothing, blankets, beads, pots, knives, and guns for furs. Many French traders married Menominee women.

More traders and settlers from Europe came to the Menominee homelands. By 1815, a trading post was built at Green Bay. Many treaties were signed to keep peace, but the Menominee were forced to give up more and more land.

CHIEF OSHKOSH

Chief Oshkosh.
A Wisconsin city has
been named Oshkosh
in honor of
this great leader.

Chief Oshkosh was made leader of the Bear Clan and chief of the Menominee in 1827.

When the Wisconsin Territory was formed in 1836, the U.S. government

29

tried to make the Menominee move west of the Mississippi River.

Chief Oshkosh did not want his people to move, but he knew the tribe needed money and supplies. So he met with U.S. officials and signed the Treaty of Cedars. Menominee land in the rich Fox River Valley was sold for 17 cents an acre, but the tribe was able to

Morning fog on the Wolf River

stay on land along the
Wolf River.

Chief Oshkosh insisted
that his people would
move no more. He helped
save the land on which
the Menominee lived, and
where they still live today. 31

SAD TIMES

President Millard Fillmore

The U.S. government expected the Menominee to start farming. But the land was sandy, swampy, and too poor for farming. And the tribe found it difficult to protect their trees from the lumber industry. In 1850, Chief Oshkosh went to Washington, D.C., to ask President Millard Fillmore to help his tribe.

Chief Oshkosh (left) worked to save the homeland of the Menominee. Today, the tribe operates a sawmill near Neopit, Wisconsin (right).

Finally, in 1854, the Menominee were given a reservation. They built homes, a church, and a school. They started a sawmill at Neopit, Wisconsin. But by 1870 war, smallpox, and other hardships had left the tribe 33

This photograph of a group of Menominee leaders was taken in 1910.

with only 1,400 members. Then a tornado hit their reservation, destroying much woodland. Later, a disease killed many pine trees. By 1950, the Menominee were struggling to survive. They had the lowest population, the least

money, and the fewest
farms in the state.

In 1953, the U.S.
government tried to put an
end to tribal organizations.
A "termination law" was
passed that caused the
Menominee hardship.
They lost their medical
care, their tribal school,
and the protection of their
own tribal laws.

Within a few years,
many Menominee lands
were sold to strangers.

The tribe was very unhappy. A group of 600 Menominee marched over 200 miles to the state capital in Madison, Wisconsin. They asked for the return of their reservation.

Finally, President Richard Nixon announced he would end the termination law. Ada E. Deer had worked on the National Committee to Save the Menominee People and Forests. Her strong voice for her

Menominee march on the
State Capitol in Madison (left).
Ada E. Deer (above) was appointed by
President Bill Clinton to the Department
of the Interior in charge of the
Bureau of Indian Affairs.

people helped restore the
rights of her tribe.

In 1973, she was chosen
leader of the Menominee
Restoration. Twenty years
later, she became the first
Native American woman to
run for the United States
Congress.

PRESENT GOVERNMENT

Today the Menominee control their reservation. Their hunting and fishing rights have been restored. They have their own police force and court system. A nine-member tribal council elects a chairman, who is like a chief. More than 500 students are taught at four schools on the reservation. The tribe has a modern clinic, a tribal office,

A Menominee church (left); a license
plate of the Menominee Nation (top right); and
the Menominee tribal police station (above)

churches, a lumber mill,
and a casino.

Most Menominee belong
to the Catholic church. But
the Great Spirit is still a
strong part of Menominee
life.

The Menominee tribal office (left) and a Menominee medical clinic in Keshena, Wisconsin

More than 3,600 Menominee live and work on the reservation, but there are not enough jobs there for everyone. Many tribal members live and work in cities throughout the Midwest.

NUCLEAR WASTE

In 1986, the U.S. government wanted to store nuclear waste on the reservation. The Menominee feared for the health of their families and their environment. Trees and land are sacred to the Menominee.

Tribal leaders successfully carried their protest to Washington, D.C. To this day, no nuclear waste has been dumped on or near the reservation.

POWWOWS

Each year during the
first weekend in August,
the Menominee Nation
holds a Powwow.

A color guard opens the annual Menominee Powwow.

Tribal singers (left) perform at the Powwow. The Powwow dance contest (inset) is very popular.

Hundreds of people come to enjoy the intertribal dance contest, the colorful costumes, and the tribal drums.

THE FUTURE

The Menominee continue to govern themselves. They are educating their children to be useful citizens of the world. But they also want their young people to know and remember the ways of their ancestors. Their native language is taught in the schools along with English.

The people work hard in their sawmill and still log in their own forests. For

Menominee wear traditional
clothing at the Powwow.

every tree they cut down,
they plant another.

The Menominee are a
proud people. With good
tribal leaders, the
Menominee nation can
look forward to a great
future. Like Spirit Rock,
they will survive forever!

WORDS YOU SHOULD KNOW

ancestors (AN • sess • terz)—grandparents or other forebears earlier in history

canoe (kuh • NOO)—a small boat made from a hollowed-out log or from a wooden frame covered with sheets of bark

cattail (KAT • tail)—a tall green plant that grows in wet places

cereal (SIR • ree • ul)—grain; a plant such as wheat and corn whose seeds are good to eat

ceremony (SAIR • ih • mo • nee)—a celebration or a religious service

clan (KLAN)—a group of related families with a common ancestor

clinic (KLIN • ik)—a place where people can receive medical treatment

council (KOWN • sil)—a meeting held to discuss problems and to decide a course of action

explorer (ex • PLOR • er)—a person who travels to far-off places to learn about the land and the people there

legend (LEH • jend)—a story about the past

nuclear waste (NOO • klee • er WAIST)—dangerous waste products from nuclear power plants

phratry (FRAT • tree)—a tribal group containing several clans

population (pop • yoo • LAY • shun)—the total number of people living in a certain place

request (rih • KWEST)—something that is asked for

reservation (rez • er • VAY • shun)—a piece of land kept as a home for American Indians

restore (rih • STORE)—to give back; to make something as it was before

sap (SAP)—the liquid that flows inside trees and carries water and nutrients to and from the leaves

sapling (SAP • ling)—a young tree with a thin trunk

settlers (SET • lerz)–people who come to a new country and establish farms or other homes there

shaman (SHAH • min)–a man or woman doctor who could cure diseases and who had close contact with the spirit world

sturgeon (STER • jun)–a large freshwater food fish of northern waters

swampy (SWAMP • ee)–wet; covered with shallow water

symbol (SIM • bil)–a thing that stands for something else

termination (ter • mih • NAY • shun)–the end of something

tobacco (tuh • BAK • oh)–a plant with broad leaves that contains a drug called nicotine

tornado (tor • NAY • doh)–a strong storm with high winds and funnel-shaped clouds

treaty (TREE • tee)–a written agreement between two groups, having to do with trade, peace, land rights, laws, etc.

tribe (TRYBE)–a group of people related by blood and customs

wigwam (WIG • wahm)–a dwelling made from a frame of poles covered with bark or mats

INDEX

About the Author

Joan Kalbacken was raised in northwest Wisconsin. She became interested in the Wisconsin Indians as she grew up with them. She received a BA in education from the University of Wisconsin, Madison, and an MA from Illinois State University in Normal, Illinois. She taught French and mathematics for twenty-nine years and served as foreign-language supervisor in Normal. She was the recipient of a "Those Who Excel" award for excellence in teaching. She is author of White-Tailed Deer *and co-author of* Recycling, Wetlands, *and* Foxes.

She is past state president of the Delta Kappa Gamma Society International and trustee of the International Educational Foundation. She is also a member of Pi Delta Phi, Kappa Delta Pi, AAUW, and Phi Delta Kappa.